The Poetic

Diary

Of

Love and Change

~Volume 2~

Clarissa O. Clemens

ISBN-13: 978-0615759531

ISBN-10: 061575953X

Hopeful Hearts Press

Table of Contents

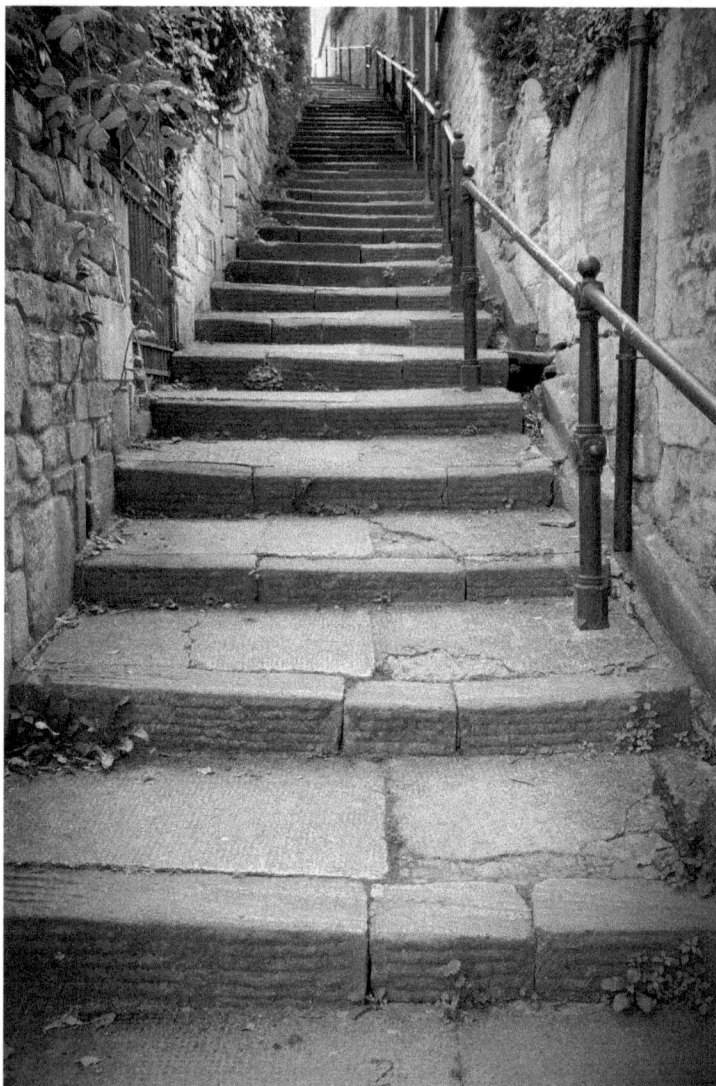

DEDICATION

This is the second volume in the series, The Poetic Diary of Love and Change. The poetry in this book was written during a tough time in my life. By writing these poems I was able to stop the tears, heal my aching heart, and feel hope for my future that I would find love once again.

I dedicate this book to anyone who has had his or her heart broken and wants to grieve, heal, and move on.

I hope my words will surround you with hope and help you to not feel alone in your sadness. I have felt your pain – have faith that love is out there waiting for you when you are ready to allow it back into your heart.

When and How

Dreaming our meeting

Into the now

Eagerly awaiting

The when and how

Do I know your name?

Where your heart resides?

Have you kept it tucked away?

So lonely it hides

I almost feel your breath,

Though we have never quite met

The smell of your skin,

The lure of your scent

Fate will find us together,

In the same place in time

Once I find you, my love,

Into your arms I will climb

Page by Page

The absence of sleep

Pushing my dreamy thoughts deep

Eyes open wide getting a good look

Opening inner visions like a treasured book

Painting with words I see inside

Page by page images start to glide

Past and future sandwich my present

Plunging further I start the descent

Falling past memories not sure how to feel

Landing on the soft core mending to heal

Deep Pond

I have left my mind

Needing you badly I find

Part of me is missing

Still longing to be kissing

Your lips tender and soft

My love for you never stops

Drifting towards the warmth of your heart

I can't stand to be away and apart

Feeling so close even by far

Hoping for light to overtake dark

The strength of our bond

Plunges me deep into your pond

Of sweet wonder my delight

Please come to me

And hold me tight

Intent and a Goal

Half my heart is incomplete

When you are around, I feel the heat

Of us together in whole desire

Bodies vibrant and on fire

The path to be whole

With intent and a goal

Driving my passion

Steering my actions

Directions seem clear

That you want me near

How close will you let me get?

I have wondered that since we met

My hope is that you are open to me

So we can find out what we will be

Slipping By

Just like that

You disappear

Just like that

You flee with fear

Fear of rejection

Fear of selection

Trust and truth

Should prevail

Seeking to soothe

Insecurity derails

Accumulated puddles

Of tears from deep

Stuck in the middle

Of a growing emotional heap

Purify with love

Can you look into my eyes?

We fit like a glove

Just the right size

If your trust in me is gone

I can't wave my magic wand

Grab hold of your inner guide

Or feel our love go slipping by

Pale Shell

The outer shell pale

Inner being fleeing

Flinch the pain

Leaping across insane

Separate apart spewing art

Single as many

Crowded with plenty

Of love to give

Descending the sieve

Cupping hands

Catching the sands

Of life eternal

Forever vernal

The joy is mine.

Caught sublime

Herds of Thoughts

What is it about words?

Rounding up thoughts like herds

Sending them throughout my bloodstream

Generating a soft sensuous dream

Potent visions so close to real

Reaching out to touch to steal

Grinning huge I can almost feel

Your skin so warm your clothes to peel

Unveil the mysterious mirage of you

Let me experience the total view

Of what it will feel to truly be

With you right here next to me

Place my Curves

I marvel at a mouth

So magnificently made

I lavish the lips

I long to lick

I harbor the heaven

Held in your hands

I bathe in the warmth

Of your breath

Can I place my curves into your angles?

Can I plunge my turquoise into your blues?

Can I rest in the rhythm of our hearts?

Can I know all the words are true?

The gift that I hold

When in your presence

The dream that I have

Of the harmony between us

The respect that we bestow

To each other's spirits

The love for you

Embrace and be near it

Clarissa O. Clemens

Swinging Gate

The glow of us together

Floating on a feather

Softly drifting through

The windswept air

Eye to eye a dreamy stare

Our heartbeats colliding in between us

Urgent need, kissing seals our trust

Comforting clouds of warm skin caressed

Words of love often suppressed

Reaching out checking your pulse

Searching your half-shut windows for clues

Realizing my door has been closed

Not allowing myself to be exposed

Trying to find my way to our fate

Walking through love's swinging gate

Ebb and Glow

Warmth flowing over

My body like melted wax

Dripping seeping helping

Me to relax

Eyelids so droopy

Lashes lowered down

Blocking out vision,

Movement, and sound

Slipping out of my body

Peeling back the glove

Floating weightless

Lifting from above

Freedom of movement

Where should I go?

Gravitating towards

That ebb and glow

Pushing the limits

Of what can be done

Tremendous senses

Searching for fun

Blurry Highs

Sloping green

Blowing serene

Waking from a dream

Things weren't what they seemed

Opening up my blurry eyes

Letting go of heavy sighs

Forming new important ties

Riding dizzy lows and highs

Arriving balanced on my feet

The thought of you, my ultimate treat

Side by side I feel complete

The peak of life the moment we meet

Cleanse and Repair

Pigeon-holed

Gathering mold

Take flight

Give up the fight

Gripping free

Take hold of me

Cleanse the soul

Repair the holes

Left by you

Leaving askew

Tripping on thoughts

Pole-vault over knots

Tied in my stomach

Burning the wick

Time passes on

Negativity gone

Past Current Future

Relaxed sublime

There isn't time

Effort gone

Full release

Sweet connection

Bittersweet reflection

Core deep surrender

Radiating splendor

Your voice a song

In my heart

Apart together

Floating smooth

Lovingly soothe

Rigid muscles

Soft current

Past words

Future pathway

Direction forward

Fingertips reaching

Barely touching

Full feelings

Creeping in

Spreading out

Wide and wishing

Letting God in

Exhilaration sweeping

Over my being

Beaming to be

Joyful and free

Clarissa O. Clemens

Dream World

Life force encapsulated during waking state

Released in dreams an eager wait

Free-flowing wonders at fingertips

Luminous flower doing flips

Streaming being breaking through gaps

Imaginary wings furiously flap

Shooting through ceilings

Peeling back the feelings

Diving into blue waters

Floating on my back like an otter

Lucidity easily broken

Tender words delicately spoken

Other worlds completely open

A place to go a place for coping

Dream world

Fondle My Heart

Ignite me

Love, a spark

Excite thee

Take you in the dark

Fondle my heart

With your loving words

We are never really apart

The fine line of reality blurs

Shutters of energy waves

Send goose bumps over my skin

Reminding me of the path we pave

To which we are destined

Words can hang lame

But our touch overcomes

Knowing we are the same

Within our bodies the passion hums

Time stands between us

To reach you and meet

Finally together

The intensity of our heat

Mind body spirit

All levels achieved

I no longer fear it

Surrender, a great release

Leaving Home

Roots unearthed

Raw and re-birthed

Clumps of sadness

Cling to madness

Moving on

Attachments gone

Special trees

Beloved buried creatures

Left behind

For someone else to find

Tears of grief

Provide relief

Letting go

New roots will grow

Obtuse Tissues

Totally drained

Rearranged brain

Try to refrain

Remaining sane

Open the closed door

Sensing what's in store

Plunging towards the future

Preparing for the lure

Of unknown issues

Grabbing for tissues

Tears letting loose

Feeling obtuse

Regaining stability

Fighting off futility

Leaning on your strength

Keeping sadness at arm's length

Ultimate truth

Love sees you through

Love of God

Love of Self

Balanced in health

Warm Tear of Sad

Something is wrong

We haven't talked in so long

Where could you be?

Why haven't you called me?

I'm missing you so bad

Warm tear of sad

Drips down my cheek

It's you that I seek

Sending you my thoughts

The love that you've brought

To my life now full

Without you is dull

I need to hear your voice

I want to be your choice

Roll my name from your lips

Feel your kiss as it dips

Into my soul making me feel whole

Creamy Dream

Warmth of sun

Rest on my shoulders

Melting thoughts

Feeling bolder

A future new

Life's adventure

Seeking balance

Risky venture

Take my hand

Touch my skin

Sense my need

Move within

Open to your

Loving advance

Creating the opportunity

For our chance

Invitation open and enticing

A creamy dream

Lapping up the icing

Lifelong longing

Anxious and prolonging

Sliding past

Slippery sensation

Lips locked tight

Tears of delight

Nirvana in sight

Sumptuous Song

Silky sliding sumptuous song

Weaving wandering winding along

Caressing ears gliding inside

Picking up moods I have never tried

Touching nerves erogenous zones

Imagining body rhythms not alone

Tense and tight soft delight

Draped fabric falling from sight

Relaxed fluidity curving intertwined

Linking languorous limbs supine

Tangled thoughts intrepid mind

Full surrender I will find

Connective perceptive

Two souls collected

One

Mirage

If I were to concentrate

hard enough

Could I wish

my old life back?

Would it manifest

as a wavering reality?

One that I thought I knew

Or would it recreate

as it really was

And send me

Down the same path

To exactly where I am now?

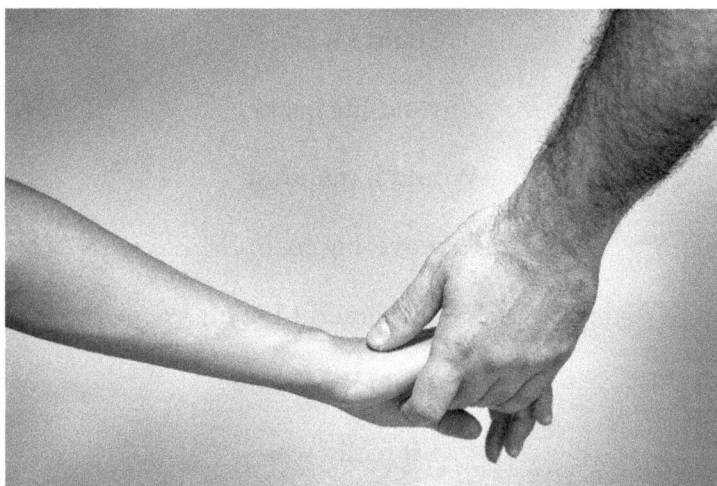

Life's Treasure

Fantastic fantasy

Majestic man

Generous and gentle

Love me when you can

My find of a lifetime

A treasure to be sure

Qualities assembled

Perfection secured

Linking fingers

Get ready for the ride

Our journey into joy

Together we will fly

Dream Beams

Incredulous lucid colorful dreams

Caressing my heart shooting out beams

Of love of light so calm so right

Soaring through clouds of cosmic desire

Pulling me out of the dredges of mire

Creating countless continuous schemes

Floating propelling weightless down the stream

Of life so cryptic yet obvious to see

I've almost reached the edge of reality

Soft Conform

Tripping on the thought without

Slipping tongues

See my pout

Sludge of time

Dragging by

Eager urge

Propelling sighs

Close my eyes

See your face

Touch my lips

Tender trace

Full and warm

Soft conform

Emerging fluid

Love is born

Find the Treasure

The power of the mind

Stuck in reverse

Now I'm lost and cannot find

What I should do first

Pulling back looking for a new view

Pushing forward my plan has gone askew

Redirecting the path for the future

Searching within to find the treasure

Option one or two, trying to decide

When the old dream of what would be has died

Leaning, locating, finding a new vision

Hoping I make the right decision

Expanding my mind to be open to more

To get ready and set for what is in store

Present Sensation

Choosing between tasks at hand

Pleasure or pain back to demand

Prefer creation not annihilation

Destroy the past present sensation

Culling cliché lines of lust

Digging deep to find the trust

Finalize the chapter completely won

Triumphant strong in search of fun

Faced with requirements to reach results

Prolong mundane ignored insults

Fresh outlook and newness permeates

Burying negative remembrance

Open the gates

Clarissa O. Clemens

Wicked Wishes

Tremendous turbulent

tantalizing twist

Taking my tongue

twirling resist

Warm wandering

wielding wonder

Wicked wishful

waking ponder

Succulent slip

my fingers awaken

Touching your skin

I am so taken

By your being

sweet and sincere

Opening my heart

attempts with no fear

Hazy head

hurling future

Glancing sideways

blurry suture

Sewing the gaps

of reality together

Holding the present

from falling apart

Through holes of tranquility

I stop to start

Right then Wrong

Another loss

Why did this have to end?

What is the cost?

Of the love that I send

Timing was right

Then went wrong

I still have my faith

For you I still long

Please take the steps

To get to me

I won't give up hope

If it's meant to be

Waves of Resolve

Flitting frenzied

harried high

Same old structure

lasting sigh

Collapse the past

Reconstruct so fast

New players in action

Cornered satisfaction

Strength gathered

flowing sea

Waves of resolve

coming over me

Relaxed motion

creates commotion

Nervous energy

propelling key

Roller coast through life

Clarissa O. Clemens

Ups and downs

blurring strife

Keel me real me

reeling blind

Open to whatever

I need to find

Match Me

Will there be someone

Who can match me?

Fulfill the need

So strong

So long

Overpower

Urgent desire

Body on fire

Who has the drive?

To keep alive

The passion surges

Endless procurement

Expectation so high

Surrender

Don't try

Clarissa O. Clemens

Setting the Stage

Don't pay attention to the first page

It's just setting the stage

For the next chapter in my life

Living on the sharp edge of the knife

Adventures unfolding

The dream of me I'm holding

Cutting through the crap

Resting my head in your lap

Always on the cusp of creating

Deep strong urges elating

Driving me on and in

I'm all ready to begin!

Silent Seasons

With every memory came

Nothing felt the same

Reflected on abstract times

Vignettes of life just pantomimes

Silent seasons slice the pie

Cutting section tears in eye

Peace to achieve

Love to relieve

Crushed under circumstance

Awkward rhythmic dance

Tripping on obstacles

Nothing's impossible

Overcome darkness

Leave behind starkness

Straightforward not bent

Straight into your arms I am sent

Grab for safety out of harm

Falling under your spell and charm

Just Words

I was thinking of writing

But then its just words

Sometimes silly

The rhyming absurd

I put the pen

snug between my fingers

And watched the letters fall down

They stuck to the paper

Piling into a mound

Labeled a poem

Anything will do

Creating mini epics

A pot of word stew

Clarissa O. Clemens

A Book For Your Healing

Writing is not only Ms. Clemens' art and passion but has also been her therapy. During times of sadness for love that faded away, she turned to her writing as a form of therapy to help process the emotions that filled her head and heart. In Volume 2 of The Poetic Diary of Love and Change, she shares more of the poems that she wrote during this transitional time so that you might also process and mend your broken heart.

The poems in this book are a therapeutic diary of love and change. They helped Clarissa to let go, grieve, and feel the hope that propelled her back into love.

This collection of poems is here to help you heal, hold on to all of your hope, and find your way back to love everlasting.

www.ingramcontent.com/pod-product-compliance
Lightning Source LLC
Chambersburg PA
CBHW060539030426
42337CB00021B/4345